Common Worship

Marriage

Charles Read

Tutor in Liturgy and Systematics, Cranmer Hall,
St John's College, Durham

Anna de Lange

Member of the Liturgical Commission

GROVE BOOKS LIMITED
RIDLEY HALL RD CAMBRIDGE CB3 9HU

Contents

Acknowledgements

We would like to thank those who have commented on parts of this booklet—especially Carolyn Headley, Trevor Lloyd, Gilly Myers and John Waller. Charles would like to thank his wife, Judith, for typing much of his contribution and staff and students (especially Dave Maher) at Cranmer Hall with whom he has discussed marriage issues over the past year.

The Cover Illustration is by Peter Ashton

First Impression February 2001
ISSN 0144-1728
ISBN 1 85174 455 X

1
New Services for Old

With a bit of imagination and the help of some background material, we can work out what a Communion service would have been like in Corinth at the time of Paul. The same process would help us to picture ourselves at a baptism around about the year 200 in a town in Eastern Europe. But we cannot do the same thing for weddings. We know that getting married and marking this with a public ceremony is a very ancient practice but we do not have any evidence that there was a specifically Christian wedding service for the first few hundred years of the church's life.

Christians seem to have used the secular (Roman) wedding ceremony and then maybe to have invited a minister to bless their relationship. Even this was not a universal custom among Christians and it is only by the ninth century that we can begin to see a specifically Christian wedding service in place in Western Europe. The wedding service evolves in the West more or less in the following way:

- *Up to tenth century:* betrothal and marriage services took place at home with a priest present.
- *Tenth to fifteenth centuries:* the marriage ceremony took place at the church door and was followed by Mass in church.
- *Sixteenth century:* Cranmer and other Reformers held the entire service in church.
- *Council of Trent [Date?]* insisted that Catholics marry in a public service; couples were forced to take this route rather than being able to marry at home as had previously been the case.
- *1753 Hardwicke Act:* English Law no longer recognized Common Law marriage and insisted that all couples marry in a public ceremony approved by the State.
- *1836 Marriage Act:* Free Church couples and Catholics in England were allowed to get married in their own churches rather than having to go to the Church of England.

It will be seen from this brief historical outline that the movement in the Western church has been from an optional celebration of marriage at home to a mandatory celebration of marriage in church. All obvious traces of the domestic setting of marriage services disappeared long before the churches of the West began liturgical revision in the twentieth century.

It will be interesting to see what effect recent legal changes will have, with the increasing fashion for weddings in stately homes, on Caribbean beaches and in other rather more unconventional locations such as hot air balloons. It is up to the church to make Christian marriage an attractive option—it no longer has a near-monopoly on good locations for the photographs.

Church of England Marriage Then and Now

Book of Common Prayer (1662): Cranmer made few changes to the medieval marriage service, parts of which were already in English anyway. What he did do was remove any hint that marriage is to be regarded as a sacrament.[1] There are no Bible readings in his marriage service because he envisaged that it would be followed immediately by Holy Communion, which would be a full service including the readings and a sermon. This expectation was unrealistic, and by the time we get to the 1662 version of his Prayer Book we find that the instruction for communion to follow the marriage service has been watered down into the rubric 'It is convenient that the new-married persons should receive the Holy Communion at the time of their Marriage, or at the first opportunity after their Marriage.' This no doubt reflected the fact that people were reluctant to add a communion service onto the marriage service and that receiving communion was not anyway as common a practice as Cranmer desired.[2]

Series 1: this marriage service appeared in 1966 and was a revised version of the marriage service in the proposed 1928 *Prayer Book.* It is still a legal option for Church of England weddings, and is authorized for use until 2005. Like the BCP, it is in 'thee' and 'thou' language but unlike the BCP allows you to omit the word 'obey' from the vows. In many ways it is not greatly different from the BCP marriage service, but is often what is meant when couples talk to the minister about having 'the traditional service.'

ASB 1980: it is debatable whether the ASB was a huge change from the BCP tradition of marriage services. It seemed quite different, being in contemporary language and having a rewritten preface setting out the reasons for getting married, but was not a radical departure in structure from the BCP. It is of course no longer a legal option for Church of England weddings.

Common Worship: the marriage service as it appears in *Common Worship* is again broadly within the BCP tradition in terms of structure and so a cynic might argue that nothing has changed since the Middle Ages! There have been a number of important changes along the way, but nothing radical such as reviving the domestic rites which accompanied medieval weddings. Early in the process it was suggested that there might be more provision for 'staged rites' and the inclusion of symbolism. However, the House of Bishops was not keen on this option and it is fair to say that opinion within the Church of England generally was divided as to whether a more creative marriage service was desirable or necessary.

1   As is made explicit in Article 25.
2   See Andrew Burnham's introduction to *Using Common Worship: Marriage* (CHP, 2000) pp 6–8.

What is Marriage?

It may be worth noting that there has been a subtle shift in understanding and defining marriage from the medieval services to the present day. The medieval view (in the West) was that marriage is a *sacrament*. As we noted above, Cranmer deconstructs this view and the ideas of marriage as *covenant* and *contract* become central. *Common Worship* sees marriage as a *gift* and *blessing* from God and as reflecting the *Trinity* (seeing the Trinity as primarily a relationship of mutual love). This is not to say that covenant ideas are absent from *Common Worship* marriage, but the more prominent concept is that of gift.

Steps and Stages

The wedding day is often described as 'the big day' and getting married is certainly a big event in anyone's life. There will have been months of planning and there will have been a growing together in love and understanding on the part of the couple. Afterwards there will be a lifetime of growing in marriage, which may include setting up home together for the first time and the gift of children. Although the wedding day is very important, it is not the whole story about getting married or being married. Yet nowadays this is the only point at which the couple's experience is likely to interact with a Christian church (unless they seek baptism for their children) if they are not members of the congregation. In earlier centuries there was more of a sense of the local church accompanying people in stages on this journey. In medieval England it was quite common for there to be a betrothal ceremony and, after the wedding itself, for there to be a blessing of the couple's new home.[3]

Many areas of life are like this. The Dutch anthropologist Arnold van Gennep wrote about rites of passage such as initiation into society, the transition from childhood into adulthood and so forth. He neatly analysed such events into three stages: separation, liminality and incorporation. Separation and incorporation are fairly easy to understand—separating yourself from your previous state of life and joining the new one. Liminality is that in-between stage when you are changing over from one thing to another. Where clergy are trained in a residential college, it is fairly easy to see the time of college training as liminality, when students feel themselves to be no longer quite laity but not yet clergy.

Common Worship, like many modern Western liturgies, makes use of this kind of anthropological theory. Liturgists talk about 'staged rites,' by which they mean providing liturgy to accompany people on their journey. Thus the Roman Catholic Church has revived the Catechumenate for baptism in which initiation is seen as a process with stages, albeit with water baptism as the indispensable focus. This fits quite well with some contemporary models of

---

3   See the section on the history of marriage in *Common Worship Today* edited by Mark Earey, Gilly Myers, Colin Buchanan and Trevor Lloyd (HarperCollins, 2001).

evangelism and nurture.[4]

The *Common Worship* funeral rites follow a staged rites approach, but the marriage service does not. There are no liturgies for engagement/betrothal and nothing for the setting up of a new home, though there is material for thanksgivings which might be used in a wedding anniversary service. In this booklet, we explore how a 'staged rites' approach to marriage might work, though to do so we have to draw on material which is not in *Common Worship*. As with staged approaches to funeral services, not every family will want to use every part of the process, but the local church's ministry to those starting out in marriage could be enhanced by offering a staged approach. It is one more set of pastoral tools for the minister to use.

2
What It Is, Is This...

When a couple approaches a minister to arrange a wedding, their expectations and perceptions are probably very different to those from the minister.

The couple may be nervous and may not have been anywhere near a church in ages. They half expect the worship to be dull, the people old and unfriendly and the minister an oddball. At least they will not have to go to a service before the big day (or will they?). For them, this step of approaching the church is the next step in their life together—much planning for the wedding has already been done and the engagement may have been celebrated some time ago.

The minister may be delighted that someone wants a church wedding, especially if the parish has few weddings. Nevertheless, he or she may regard their arrival on the doorstep as another interruption in a busy day. There may be logistical questions: can we fit them in more or less when they want, especially if the parish has many weddings? Perhaps there are ethical questions: has one of them been married before? or can I in all conscience charge these fees when the couple are both unemployed? There may be mission questions (how can I draw these two people to faith?), or pastoral questions raised by talking about family relationships.

The situation may be further complicated if the first point of contact for the couple is with the parish secretary or the minister's spouse. Since first impressions are so important, it is worthwhile reflecting on how best to han-

---

4   Especially *Emmaus* courses—see the rationale in the introduction to Steve Croft, Felicity Lawson, Stephen Cottrell and Robert Warren, *Emmaus: The Way of Faith.[publn details?]*

dle these initial inquiries. If the minister holds a 'surgery hour' how should it be publicised? Or if the first contact is by telephone or e-mail, the couple can be encouraged to make personal contact with the minister at a time when he or she has plenty of time for a conversation. Then there is leisure to include not just the basic details of arranging the service but also something of how getting engaged fits into their growing together as a couple.

In all this, liturgy may seem the last thing on anyone's mind. Even if there were a liturgy to celebrate engagement, it is far too late to use it in most cases. The moment passed long before the couple met the minister. The Roman Catholic Church in England and Wales has a Rite for Celebrating Engagement in its proposed *Order of Christian Marriage* (OCM), but while this may be a realistic option in some Catholic communities where the priest may be in contact with a family when engagements happen, it would be very unusual in the Church of England. The Liturgical Commission began to draft such a service, but it was not proceeded with and is not part of the *Common Worship* package. There are prayers for engagement in the very helpful but totally unofficial *Pastoral Prayers*.[5]

What realistic options are open to Church of England clergy?

1. Thanksgiving for relationships/engagements could be included in the regular Sunday worship or midweek prayer meeting. This helps to indicate that Christians are concerned about such matters and it alerts the regular congregation to the fact that couples (whom they may rarely see) get married in this church. It is important to be sensitive to the feelings of those present who have had (or are having) painful and damaging relationships, or who are single and do not particularly want to be, or who are single and feel invisible in a church which only seems to recognize families. There is useful prayer material in the Supplementary Texts section of *Common Worship: Pastoral Services* on pp 157–168, though the texts will need adapting to this kind of use. *Patterns for Worship* has suitable intercession material on pp 82–84.

2. For some couples, a simple celebration of their engagement at home or as part of a church service might be appropriate. A possible order of service might be:
   • Informal introduction by the minister.
   • Scripture reading (Psalm 144.17–18; 1 Thessalonians 3.12–13; Hosea 2.21–26 are all possibilities).
   • Prayer(s) for the couple, maybe including prayer over the engagement ring (for an example, see below).
   • The Lord's Prayer.

---

5   Edited by Richard Deadman, Jeremy Fletcher, Janet Henderson and Stephen Oliver (Mowbray, 1996)—see p 31.

- Sharing the Peace.
- Grace before the meal (if the engagement is being celebrated in the context of a celebratory meal).

3. A prayer could be said as part of the initial meeting to discuss planning/ booking the wedding. This prayer might focus on the engagement ring or on the couple growing into marriage or both. Such a prayer could also be printed on a card for the couple to take away and use themselves, and might also be used in church services where engaged couples are prayed for. Two examples are:

Creator God, you have sown in the hearts of N and N
the seeds of longing and affection that they might grow
    together in mutual trust and love.
Bless the commitment they have made to each other.
By your blessing may this ring be a sign of their hopes for each other.
Bless this time of preparation that they may rejoice with their family
    and friends on the day of their wedding
and in company with Christ our Lord. **Amen.**

Eternal God,
give your blessing to N and N
in their hopes and in their dreams.
May these come true
through their faith in each other
and their trust in you.
Teach them how great is the joy
that comes from sharing;
how deep the love that grows with giving.
Lead them in peace
to the day of their wedding
and be with them in their hearts and in their home(s)
now and for ever. **Amen.**[6]

---

6   These two prayers are from a very early draft by the Liturgical Commission. They have never been part of the Common Worship marriage rites and are copyright the Archbishops' Council. They are given here as examples only of possible styles of prayer in these circumstances. They are also found in *Pastoral Prayers* p 31.

3

Planning and Preparing

Even if the local church has not been able to be in contact with the couple at their engagement and involved with them as their love for each other grows, from the moment the wedding is booked possibilities for ministry emerge.

There are three broad areas where prayer and liturgy may come in useful.

Prayer at the Calling of Banns

Given that most congregations will not know most of the couples getting married in the church, the calling of banns can be a significant stage in the local church's ministry to engaged couples. For the first time in the Church of England, *Common Worship* provides texts for prayer at this moment (*Common Worship: Pastoral Services* p 135[7]), but there is no reason why the minister cannot make up his or her own. If the couple attend church for at least one reading of the banns (they do not have to) it might be possible, having checked with them beforehand, to ask them to stand where they are or come out to the front. The prayer could be accompanied by laying on of hands (by the minister and with others joining in)—maybe even by anointing if you (and they) are adventurous!

Where banns are not being read (because the marriage is to be by licence) it is probably desirable to invent some kind of announcing ceremony akin to calling banns. This way all couples are offered the opportunity for public prayer as part of marriage preparation. Experience indicates that where one party has been divorced, the couple can feel they are being hidden away out of shame if banns are not being called, so in this case some kind of public announcement is often pastorally desirable.[8]

Wedding Preparation

Stephen Lake rightly stresses the importance of good wedding preparation, especially the rehearsal.[9] Many parishes arrange meetings to discuss other aspects of getting and being married.[10] While the emphasis of these occasions will probably be on the practical aspects of preparing for the wedding service or on the meaning of Christian marriage, it is again possible to include some prayer and maybe a short act of worship (including a hymn) if the preparation session involves enough people (say, a marriage preparation day for several

---

7   References are to the *Common Worship: Pastoral Services* book, but the marriage service is also available as an offprinted separate.
8   Most dioceses recommend that where one party is divorced, marriage should be after Superintendent Registrar's Certificate and not the calling of banns.
9   Lake, *Using Common Worship: Marriage*, pp 25–30.
10   See M Stevens, *Preparing Couples for Marriage* (Grove Pastoral booklet P 28).

couples, which some parishes hold). A simple outline for this might be:

- Thanksgiving prayer for marriage (see *Pastoral Services* pp 161, 164).
- Hymn (or part of a hymn) celebrating marriage or seeking God's guidance.[11]
- Short Bible reading (*Pastoral Services* pp 137–149 has suggestions).
- Prayer for the couples as they prepare for marriage (perhaps one of the 'banns' prayers).

Where the preparation is with one couple (and their families) only, it is still possible to use some of this prayer material (and a Bible reading).

Prayer at Home

Parishes could print a card with suitable prayer material on it for the couple to use at home as they prepare for marriage. Some of the prayers in *Common Worship* can be adapted for this purpose, often merely by changing the pronouns to 'we' and 'us.' A candle could be lit at home and a prayer said, perhaps when the couple meet (with other family members?) to plan aspects of the wedding. This is particularly appropriate if the couple wish to use a candle at their wedding, as is becoming popular.[12] Material on pp 135, 161, 164, 166 and 168 of the *Pastoral Services* volume is a good starting point here. As with other aspects of preparation, the minister will need to adapt the provisions to the needs and aspirations of each couple. Not every couple will want to use prayers at home, but maybe this is a practice it is worth trying to encourage.

---

11 *eg Lord of all hopefulness* or *Lord for the years*—there are many general hymns which might be suitable.
12 See Charles Read, *Revising Weddings* (Grove booklet W 128) p 19 and Lake *Marriage*, p 98.

4

The Big Day

The marriage preparation has been given, the last minute panics have happened (the couple have found the cake and the page boys, the dress still fits, the best man has the rings...) and you are off to church to conduct the wedding. The *Common Worship* marriage service is not that different from the ASB, but it does provide a few new options, about which you need to be clear and to have discussed with the couple as part of the preparations. No matter how stunning the wedding preparations and pastoral care have been up to now, this is the part of the proceedings which makes the biggest impression on most people. It is important to get the service as right as possible for the couple and their families and friends.

In this chapter we go through the service step by step, pointing out the options and offering some theological insights into the new service.

It is important to note that the service has a clear structure in two sections—introduction and marriage. This reflects the medieval division between those parts of the rite that happened at the church door and those that happened inside. It also points out that the Declarations and the bride and groom's responses 'I will' are part of the preliminaries, not the marriage.

Before We Begin...

Common Worship provides a Pastoral Introduction on p 102 which can be printed at the front of an order of service or on a card to be placed in the pews. This introduction sets out something of the meaning of Christian marriage and what the congregation's role as witnesses to the marriage involves. The idea is that the congregation will read this while they wait for the service to begin; it might help them to settle, and remind them of what is about to happen.

What about the notices? Guidance about confetti, following the service in the order of service, when to take photos and so on may be given before the start of the service so that the act of worship does not begin with such details. It is worth remembering, though, that some people will be waiting outside for the arrival of the bride (and maybe the groom—see later) and will miss these announcements—so making them at the start of the service may be the lesser of two evils. You will have to weigh up which will be better in your circumstances.

The Introduction

Entrance. Common Worship allows the bride and groom to process down the aisle together. The point of this is to emphasize that the service is for the

11

couple and is not just 'the bride's day.'[13] The bride and groom come to church already as a couple. If this practice is adopted (and it is worth encouraging couples to consider it), you will need to work out who goes where in the entrance procession. Will the bride's father and the groom's best man wait at the front of the church, or will they enter behind the couple or behind the bridesmaids? Of course, the groom may still wait at the front of church and the bride may enter with her father or another male relative as is felt to be traditional (though in fact this practice is not as old as that of the couple entering church together).

Starting the Service. This is subtitled 'The Welcome' and that sums up how the tone of this part of the service should be. Nothing is mandatory at this stage of the service, but material is provided for the welcome and an opening prayer as well as for singing a hymn.

Preface. The opening preface sets out the purpose of marriage and of the service. A new one has been written for *Common Worship* although a revised version of the ASB preface is given as an alternative (p 136). The two cover much the same ground and you and the couple need to decide which one to use. The new one has a more clearly trinitarian feel to it and also stresses the social aspects of getting married. There is a more open reference to sex than in the ASB.

The Declarations. These are not much changed from the ASB except that the possibility now exists (note 7 on p 133) for the bride to make her declaration and her vows before the groom, indicating the equality and complementarity of the couple in the sight of God. The same note also allows the use of the BCP Declarations, though without printing them in the book.

The other real innovation here is that there is a parallel question to the congregation, asking the families and friends of the couple if they will 'support and uphold them in their marriage now and in the years to come?' This question to the congregation is not optional and reflects a recognition of the role of the guests in the lives of the couple, a wish to give the congregation a more active role in the service and a desire to acknowledge that married couples need the support of those around them. The couple's parents can also express their support at this stage (see the 'giving away' below).

The Collect, Readings and Sermon. All three elements are mandatory, although only one Bible reading need be used. A selection of suggested readings is offered on pp 137–149. The ASB allowed the Ministry of the Word to come either here or at a later point in the service, after the marriage had taken place. *Common Worship* very strongly prefers this earlier position so that the marriage can take place 'in the light of Scripture.' In other words, the structure of the service assumes that some teaching will be given on the nature of Christian marriage before the congregation and the couple proceed to the marriage itself. Obviously, chairs will need to be provided for the couple, bridesmaids,

---

13 See Charles Read, *Revising Weddings*, p 8f.

bride's father and so on and different church buildings will lend themselves to different specific arrangements. This is one of the points where rehearsal before the day with the people involved, so that everyone can move smoothly to their seats, could be so important to the success of the whole service. Some people have worried that having the readings and the sermon in this position will mean that no-one actually listens to them because everyone is anxious to get on with the wedding. In fact, many couples may welcome the opportunity to sit down and simply listen at this stage in the service—it may actually help to calm their nerves. Only time will tell if this will work better than having the readings and sermon later in the service.

The Marriage

The 'Giving Away.' The main text of the service does not mention this ceremony at all. The giving away is possibly the last vestige of the notion of the bride being her father's property and being handed over to another man to become his property.[14] Experience shows that modern couples recoil in horror when it is pointed out that the giving away of the bride historically depicts the woman as property but nonetheless they want to keep the ceremony 'because it is traditional.' *Common Worship* has a bold attempt at re-working this tradition, not simply ridding it of its patriarchal overtones but enabling it to carry a message of the couple being supported by their families.

The note on p 133 explains it all. If the giving away is to be done at all, it can be done in one of two ways. The traditional way is before the vows, with the bride being presented by her father or another person representing the family. The alternative form takes place earlier in the service, after the couple have made their declarations (p 106) and before the question is put to the congregation. Parents of both bride and bridegroom are asked to entrust their children to one another as they come to be married. This has some parallels with the idea of sponsorship at baptism. It might also serve to underline that, in marriage, both a man and a woman loosen ties with their parents in order to unite with each other—the 'leaving and cleaving' of Genesis 2.24.

The Vows. There are actually four versions of the vows, two in contemporary language and two in traditional language. In one form of each the bride promises to obey her husband, and in the other form she does not.[15] The choice of forms can now be made on the basis of a preference for language, as well as for the wording of the vows. It is part of the *Common Worship* ethos that old and new can be held together in one book and in one service. The main provision as set out on p 108 is a contemporary language version without the promise to obey. The other options can be found on pp 150–151.

---

14 See *Revising Weddings*, p 8.
15 In the contemporary version, 'obey' is no longer mirrored by 'worship.'

We have already seen that note 7 on p 133 allows the bride to make her vow first. The logistics of how the vows are made remain unchanged from the ASB and the BCP. A rubric encourages the bride and groom to face each other and hold hands—they are making the vows to each other and not to the minister. They may repeat the vows line by line after the minister, they may read the vows from a card or they may learn the words and recite them. The first option is the safest and commonest while the third option is probably the most powerful and dramatic.

The Giving of Rings. There are two prayers which can be used when the minister receives the rings (on pp 109 and 151). As in the ASB, there is provision for the couple to exchange rings or for there to be just one ring. A note allows to couple to say the words '*N*, I give you this ring...' together.[16]

The Proclamation. This is unchanged from the ASB except that *Common Worship* brings back from the BCP the word 'asunder.' The ASB phrase 'let not man divide' was unnecessarily exclusive in its language but was easily modified into 'let no-one divide.' While some may feel that Andrew Burnham's suggestion that the word is still in common use is an overstatement,[17] there was agreement on the Revision Committee that this point in the service required some solemnity and weight, which is more easily achieved with the four syllables of 'put asunder' than with the two of 'divide.' Aside from these linguistic matters, there is perhaps the possibility of adding to the service here by using some symbolic action such as anointing the couple or binding their hands together with the minister's stole. This may also be the point at which the wedding candle is lit, if this custom is to be introduced.[18]

The Blessing of the Marriage. It was very unclear whether there was an official nuptial blessing in the ASB marriage service. The prayer for the blessing of the couple did not look like a classic nuptial blessing whereas the one prayer which did look like one was just an option in the appendix of possible intercessions. *Common Worship* rectifies this by providing five or six nuptial blessings. If versions 3, 4 or 5 in the supplementary texts on pp 153–155 are used, they need to be printed out so that the congregation can join in with the appropriate responses. The versicles and responses which begin 'Blessed are you, heavenly Father' may be used on their own or may be added to any of the other forms (see p 155). All these nuptial blessings are optional. However, the 'blessing proper' towards the bottom of p 111 must be used in all cases.

The Registration of the Marriage. It makes best sense to register the marriage at this point in the service because it is the legal counterpart of the blessing and proclamation of the marriage. After the couple have exchanged vows, the church and the State (both represented by the minister in Church of England weddings) take over. The couple have been the ministers of marriage to each

---

16 Note 8, p 133.
17 In Stephen Lake, *Using Common Worship: Marriage*, p 17.
18 For more on these and other symbolic acts see Lake, *Marriage*, pp 96–99 and C Read, *Revising Weddings*, pp 17–20.

other (they marry each other, they are not—strictly speaking—married by the minister). Now the church asks God to bless their marriage and the State registers it. To keep this parallel between blessing and registration, it is helpful if the registration can take place in church in full view of the congregation. Nevertheless some churches will not have a suitable space for this to be done and the wedding party will have to retire to a vestry or hall.

Registrars prefer the registers to be filled in from scratch at this point, to avoid the possibility of confusion if one party fails to turn up or dies before the marriage is complete (it does happen!). However, it saves time during the service and is a safe precaution if the registers are filled out before the service begins; this needs both adequate time and freedom from distractions. The marriage register contains full instructions on how to fill it in, including what to do if a mistake is made. The groom or best man should arrive early enough on the day to check the registers before the service.

Some clergy satisfy the need of some members of the congregation to take photographs by providing an opportunity to do so at the signing of the registers. In this case, the couple and their witnesses should sign the registers without the distraction of being photographed, even by their official photographer. When the registers have all been signed, the photograph can be staged with only one of the registers left on the table. The bride's bouquet and a Bible may also be placed on the table for the photographs. The official photographer takes photographs first and then any other member of the congregation can come out and do the same. Some music can be played while all this is going on and experience indicates that this process need not go on for too long but is appreciated by the couple and their guests.

The Prayers. No instructions are given about where the couple sit or kneel for the prayers and much will depend upon the layout of the building and the wishes of the minister and the couple themselves. There is also a great deal of flexibility regarding the form the prayers should take. Page 112 gives a suggested sequence of themes for the prayers: thanksgiving; spiritual growth; faithfulness, joy, love, forgiveness and healing; children, family and friends. The only mandatory item is the Lord's Prayer (which will need to be printed, in either its contemporary or traditional form). Sample prayers are given on pp 112–113 and pp 156–168. Other material can be found in *Patterns for Worship* from p 82 (though it may need some sensitive adapting). To use some of these prayers, the congregation need to have enough of the text in front of them to be able to join in the responses. Silence may be kept, extemporary prayer may be offered and prayers may be used which the couple have written or chosen. Although this is not specified in the service, it might sometimes be appropriate for couples to lead part of the prayers themselves.[19]

The Dismissal. The service ends with a blessing of the congregation. The text does not give any instructions on how to get the couple out of the church but this matter does need a bit of careful planning. Different buildings will suggest different ways of doing it. For example, there is a neat way of turning the couple around: first they link arms while standing facing the front of church, then one partner walks forward and the other backward at the same time. They find themselves neatly facing the right way. The bridesmaid may need to look after the bride's train while this is going on, and a rehearsal is a good idea, made easier if the church has a mock train which can be tied around the bride's waist. Anyone whom the couple want to follow them out of church as part of the wedding party can then line up behind them and when everyone is ready, the organist can play the music for them to go out to. The couple should not stop until they get out of church (otherwise they will never get started again). Anyone who jumps out in front of them to take a photograph very soon seems to get out of the way when they realize the bridal party is not going to stop.[20]

Hymns

Various points are indicated throughout the service where hymns may conveniently be sung, but these positions are not mandatory and other possibilities exist. The supplementary texts include four possible biblical canticles and it would be good to see creative people turning these into hymns and songs for use at weddings.

Holy Communion

Thomas Cranmer envisaged that Holy Communion would follow immediately on from the marriage service but by 1662 this intention had been watered down into being merely desirable. The ASB further diluted this into a suggestion and *Common Worship* does not do very much to strengthen it again. However, it does suggest that for communicant Christians it is appropriate that they receive communion soon after their marriage and that it maybe appropriate for the marriage to take place as part of a Communion service. A worked out order for marriage within Holy Communion is given on pp 116–131. It should be noted that all the flexibility associated with both the marriage service and the service of Holy Communion can be utilized here, so there is great scope for Christian couples tailoring their marriage service to their own needs and desires.[21]

Involving others

As with other *Common Worship* services (and continuing the trend of the ASB), there is scope for involving others in leading parts of the wedding service. This is especially true of the readings and the prayers and there is an

19   See note 9, p 133.
20   For further advice on this and other aspects of the staging of the service, see Stephen Lake, *Marriage*, especially chapter 2.
21   For help and advice on these other services, see Trevor Lloyd, *A Service of the Word*, Jeremy Fletcher, *Communion in Common Worship* and Charles Read and Colin Buchanan, *The Eucharistic Prayers of Order 1*—all published in the Grove Worship series.

explicit note about ministers of other churches (which we discuss in chapter 7). The clue to watch out for is a phrase like 'These or other suitable prayers.'

Reality

Couples sometimes feel that they do not fit the standard pattern for wedding couples and some of these issues are addressed in chapter 7. Three other common areas of concern are:

1. *The Need for Penitence.* Perhaps where one party has been married before or where there is something else in the past life of the bride or groom, the couple may feel that they need to get themselves right with God before they get married. The minister can and should offer help in this area as part of the preparation for getting married, if such matters come to light in his conversations with the couple. Prayers of penitence and assurance of forgiveness can be used privately in wedding preparation conversations but may also be woven into the early part of the marriage service (maybe before the preface). Prayers of penitence are compulsory at a marriage service within a celebration of Holy Communion.

2. *Children.* The couple may have children from this or a previous relationship and it is quite common for such children to be involved in the service as bridesmaids or page boys. The *Common Worship* marriage service includes suggested prayers which also acknowledge the existence of the couple's children—see prayer 25 on p 167. The preface may also be adapted to read '...in which children are nurtured' rather than 'born and nurtured.' For some couples there is the knowledge that they are very unlikely to have children. In this case, texts can be adapted so that they omit references to the gift of children—this is usually indicated by a paragraph being enclosed in square brackets—there are examples on pp 157 and 159.

3. *Fragility.* Most couples and most wedding congregations are all too aware that being married is not easy and that many marriages do not last. Will this one? Such fears can be addressed in the wedding sermon and again the prayers can be used to handle this concern. (See for example prayer 13 on p 163 and prayer 18 on p 165—but many other parts of the service can be seen as linking with this concern.) The important elements to stress are the need to seek God's grace and help and the importance of sensitive and appropriate support by family and friends.

5

Bless this House

Setting up home together corresponds to getting married in three possible ways:

- the couple get married and then move away from the parish to set up home;
- the couple get married and then set up home in the parish;
- the couple are already living together when they get married.

The local church can offer a service of blessing the home in all three cases, but it will need to be adapted to the particular circumstances. In the first scenario the minister who performs the wedding ceremony will need to put the couple in touch with the clergy of the parish they are moving to. In the other two situations the minister who performed the wedding would probably be the right person to perform the house blessing. However, this is also just the kind of ministry which can be shared with lay people, especially Readers and those involved in wedding preparation.

The Church of England does not provide official texts and services for these kinds of occasions. Many dioceses do have services for the blessing of a new home and it is also perfectly possible to invent your own—but if there is a service available which you can use or adapt, then why not start with that? One such source is *Pastoral Prayers*[22] which contains a suggested form of service and prayers for various rooms of the house on pp 5–9.

The suggestion below is based partly on this book and partly on prayers being considered by the Roman Catholic Church in England and Wales.

An Outline Structure
- Greeting [and sharing the Peace].
- Introduction to the service.
- Bible reading.
- Prayer in various rooms in the house.
- Other prayers, including the Lord's Prayer and prayer for the couple.
- [Sharing of the Peace and] Blessing.

Some Considerations
Who should be involved? The minister may be lay or ordained and the couple should be encouraged to lead parts of the service and to share in preparing it. Family, friends and neighbours could be invited and the service ought to be kept fairly informal. It would be good to follow it with a party!

22 See page 7 above.

What reading to use? It might be a passage about Jesus sharing in the hospitality of someone's home (Luke 19.1–9; John 1.35–39—a passage like Luke 10.38–42 [Martha and Mary at home] needs careful handling) or hospitality in the OT (Genesis 18.1–10).

Prayers around the house. It is possible to find biblical allusions for many rooms and a brief prayer can be written based on such a passage each time.

For example, here is a prayer for the kitchen from the draft *Order for Christian Marriage*:

O God, you fill the hungry with good things.
Send your blessings on us, as we work in this kitchen
and make us ever thankful for our daily bread.

And here is its equivalent from *Pastoral Prayers:*

Grant, Lord, to all who shall work in this room that in serving others they may serve you and share in your perfect service, and that in the busyness of the kitchen they may possess you in tranquillity, through Jesus Christ our Lord.

It is important to compose these prayers carefully and they should be brief. You probably do not need a new prayer for each bedroom, especially if the house is a seven bedroomed Victorian vicarage!

Action and symbolism. Some people might want to accompany the prayers around the house with sprinkling with holy water. If the local congregation has bought the couple a small wedding present (such as a Bible), it could be placed in the home as part of this service. Likewise, if a candle has been used as part of the wedding ceremony, it could be lit as part of this service.[23]

Cohabitation

The fact of cohabitation raises ethical questions for many Christians, including those who might be leading weddings and blessings of homes. There are a range of possible responses to this. Ignoring the fact of cohabitation and carrying on as if the couple were not living together already might be seen as the church being embarrassed by this and ignoring it. At the opposite end of the scale, making the couple go through some high profile act of repentance runs the risk of implying that sexual sin is so serious it needs dealing with separately; we do not after all make such a fuss about other sins the couple may be committing. Perhaps a general act of confession and absolution would be helpful in most wedding ceremonies. This is the kind of issue which a church staff meeting needs to discuss to work out an agreed policy and practice.[24]

---

23 See Charles Read, *Revising Weddings*, pp 17–20 and Lake, *Marriage*, pp 96–99.
24 See further on this subject Gary Jenkins, *Cohabitation: A Biblical Perspective* (Grove booklet E 84).

6
When I'm Sixty-Four

Anniversaries come and go, and sometimes a couple might celebrate them with a meal, or a weekend away from the kids. Sometimes they are 'big ones,' such as ten, twenty-five or fifty years. Sometimes they are significant for other reasons—maybe the couple have had a rocky time over the past year, and doubted whether they would reach the anniversary together.

Many churches try to keep in contact with baptism families. They send birthday cards or anniversary of baptism cards to the child, and encourage the parents and godparents to bring the child to church and to children's groups. Some invite all those who have been recently baptized for The Baptism of Christ. It is also common for there to be an annual service for funeral families, usually at All Souls.' Relatively few churches try in this structured way to maintain links with couples who were married in their church, and yet the opportunity is there to encourage spiritual growth.

- A young couple may have enjoyed and been touched by their experience of worship, but be embarrassed to return ('we feel we just used the church'): issue invitations for a celebration service and that gives the opening for a return visit.
- There might be a good reason (such as occurred with the Queen's golden wedding) to invite couples who were married in a certain year to come back and reaffirm their vows.
- If a couple have been through a hard time and have come to the church for help or comfort there are possibilities for pastoral liturgy in a renewal of vows.
- Some couples feel that a party is good for most anniversaries, but a silver or golden one deserves a bit more, and maybe returning to church and to the presence of God.

Common Worship provides a suggested form of service which can be adapted for use on any of these and other occasions. An introductory note spells out that the service does not even have to be in church. Indeed, if a couple want to mark a reconciliation by reaffirming their vows it might well be more appropriate to have a low-key ceremony at home, maybe combining it with prayers for the home and for the family. On the other hand, Epiphany might be a suitable time for a special new year celebration, with the wedding at Cana featuring in the second service readings.

The provision (pp 184 onwards) comes in the form of an Outline Order along the principles of a Service of the Word, followed by a Sample Service that illustrates one way of amplifying the Order, for a major church occasion. The Outline Order deliberately echoes the shape of the marriage service, and couples can be encouraged to use the same texts as in their marriage.

The service opens with a welcome, an opening prayer and possibly a hymn. There follows a Preface which carries echoes of both the ASB and the *Common Worship* prefaces. Two phrases are bracketed, and the decision to include or exclude them needs pastoral sensitivity. The first speaks of asking forgiveness for all that has been amiss in the marriage, and a footnote hints that this will not always be appropriate. However, 'it may be important to include it when a couple are celebrating their reconciliation.' If this is the case, it might be appropriate to add some penitential prayers (see p 175 for suggested texts, including one in Kyrie form) either before or after the readings and sermon. The second pause for thought is three lines concerning children. Many have no problem with affirming the family as a purpose of marriage, but for others the whole issue of children is intensely painful. This could be a point when some exploration of the liturgy by the minister would reveal hurts and pains. Maybe it would provide an opportunity for pastoral ministry, for an honest appraisal of feelings by the couple and for prayer for understanding and healing of the past.

The renewal of vows looks straightforward, and for a service with only one couple it is—though they may prefer to use the exact form of vows that they used on their wedding day. In a service with several couples it would be necessary to think through the 'choreography.' Does each couple renew their vows in turn, making it possible to use the original form? Or is this to be done as a group? If the latter, which form of vows will be used, and how will you manage the opening line 'I, N, took you, N, to be my wife' (or husband)? Will all say the line in turn (if numbers are limited); or will all say it together, using the appropriate names (which will not be heard in the babble); or will you drop the use of names, relying on the fact that the couples are holding hands and facing each other to make the point? Whichever is chosen, the text and movement needs communicating (and possibly rehearsing).

What about the ring? Some couples wish to exchange new rings, such as an eternity ring; others may wish to recognize the ongoing significance of the wedding ring. Provision is made for either choice.

There follows a blessing of the couple(s), and prayers. As well as the prayer printed on p 191 there are many suitable prayers, or prayers which could be adapted, in the provision for the marriage service itself. The suggested service ends with the Lord's Prayer and a blessing. And on to the party!

We're Not Your Average Couple

Every wedding is unique, and every couple is unique. But the majority of weddings fit into the 'normal' formula, with the variety being in the the hymns and readings that the couples choose. From time to time every minister is approached by two people whose wedding does not quite fit into the norm. What then?

Inter-church Weddings

'We want to get married in this church, because I come here and anyway it is my home. But John goes to the Methodist church where he lives, and where our home is going to be. We'd like the minister there to be involved in our wedding, and to use some prayers from the Methodist marriage service.'

It is a delight to marry a couple with clear Christian commitment, and their request is to be welcomed. Yet the marriage certificate has to declare that the marriage was according to the rite of the Church of England. What latitude is there for alteration? The ASB was silent, but *Common Worship* gives clear guidance, and points towards a marriage service which provides specifically for this situation.

Note 13 on p 134 of *Pastoral Services* spells out which parts of the service must be taken by the Church of England minister, and which may be led by a minister of another Christian church. In summary, the Church of England minister must establish that there is no impediment, direct the vows, declare the existence of the marriage, say the final blessing and sign the registers. All other parts of the service, including some or all of the Preface, the Sermon, the Declarations, the Giving of Rings and the Blessing of the Marriage can be led by the other minister.

The same note also cites *An Order for the Marriage of Christians from Different Churches*, which the bishop may authorize to be used. This Order was prepared by the Joint Liturgical Group, and was authorized in Synod as part of this set of rites, and thereby became a legal rite of the Church of England for the purposes of the marriage certificate. The decision was taken, however, that it would not be published in the *Pastoral Services* volume.[25] The Order differs in both structure and text from the *Common Worship* marriage service. It is shaped more like a Communion service and uses forms of declaration and vows which are legally required for Roman Catholic and Free Church marriages in England and Wales.

So the answer to our couple can be 'No problem. We can work out the form of service and how we can involve John's minister when you come to see me next.'

Inter-faith Weddings

Many couples who come from different religious backgrounds are aware of the questions this raises about having a specifically and solely Christian wedding

---

25 It is available separately from Canterbury Press (1999, ISBN 1 85311 309 3).

service. Often they will opt for a civil wedding, but sometimes a minister will receive a request from such a couple for a wedding in church. No inter-faith wedding ceremony has ever been authorized by the Church of England and this scenario is perhaps the most difficult to deal with. The following are offered as initial guidelines, but carry no official weight whatsoever! It is probably wise to refer all requests for inter-faith weddings to the bishop as soon as possible.

- Anyone living in the parish has a right to a first wedding in the parish church, even if they do not profess the Christian faith.
- The *Common Worship* marriage service is a Christian service; Church of England wedding services must be clearly Christian. (And this is what parishioners have a right to—their right is not simply to a wedding service but to a Church of England one).
- It is possible to include a reading from a non-biblical source—but at least one Bible reading must be used. (Care needs to be taken here to avoid implying that Christians see other holy books as 'just like the Bible').
- It may be possible to include symbolism from other cultures or religions—this is where the use of flowers and crowns comes from in Indian Christian weddings. (But again, care needs to be taken here—what is such symbolism saying? Some symbols 'transfer' from one religion to another, as in the flower and crown examples; others may not).
- Prayer together may be possible—but opens up a whole range of questions about whether Christians can meaningfully pray with those of other faiths.[26]

Marriage of Divorced People

One of the most common 'discoveries' upon first contact with an engaged couple is that one or both of them is divorced, and with a previous spouse still living. The Church of England continues to tie itself in knots over this issue. Practice varies from diocese to diocese, from parish to parish and indeed from minister to minister. At the same time that the *Common Worship* services were going through Synod a Working Party of the House of Bishops was drafting a discussion document, published in 2000 as *Marriage in Church after Divorce*.[27]

At the time of writing, no final decision have been made, but the Revision Committee was very conscious that the report was in preparation. They endeavoured to draft the new service in such a way that it would be possible to use it for a wedding involving a divorced person, while not undermining the church's current understanding of the doctrine of marriage.

Also included in the *Pastoral Services* volume is a light revision of *An Order for Prayer and Dedication after a Civil Marriage* (pp 173–183). The original was a service which did not appear in the ASB, but which was commended for use by the House of Bishops and published as a separate booklet. Sometimes, when one partner

---

26   For help on questions of inter-faith worship generally see D Bookless, *Inter-Faith Worship* (Grove booklet W 117) and the official Church of England report *Multi-Faith Worship?* (CHP, 1992).

27   GS1361—sometimes called the Winchester Report.

has been divorced, the couple may want prayers of penitence to be included in the service, and suitable optional prayers are included after the Preface (p 174).[28] The service is deliberately and clearly not a marriage. The couple enter church 'together without ceremony' (note 3, p 183); the Dedication (p 177) carries echoes of the declarations and the vows in the marriage service without being a word-for-word replication; there is a prayer for the rings already given and worn, but not an exchange of rings. The blessings present a bewildering contradiction. The options for the blessing of the couple (p 178) include the Aaronic 'priestly' blessing but may be led (in 'you' form, as no other makes sense) by a deacon or even apparently a lay minister.[29] The blessing of the congregation has an italicized *you* throughout for those who prefer to use the 'we' form, but must be replaced by The Grace (note 5) when the service is not led by a ordained presbyter! There is the further complication that the church appears here to bless a marriage which it would not solemnize in the first place. If one of the functions of the marriage service is to bless the marriage, how is this service theologically different?

Appendix: Orders of Service

Not everybody wants, or can afford, to have personalized orders of service printed. Not every church wants, or can afford, to buy the marriage separates. So what is to be done about congregational texts?

The only mandatory response for the congregation is 'We will' in the Declarations, and on all but the most formal occasions the minister can prompt the necessary words as part of the introduction to the service or to that part of it. Yet even then the Lord's Prayer is always said (and even among regular churchgoers the variant versions can be a source of confusion) and there are various options with responses that the couple might choose.

You could produce a brief order of service containing the Pastoral Introduction (p 102), the structure of the service (p 103), the text of the congregational question and response (p 106), and one or both versions of the Lord's Prayer (p 113). This gives security to those who want to know where in the service they are, and texts for the essential parts so that the congregation can join in. It can be offered to couples at an early stage of their wedding preparation, with an explanation that any other choices they make could necessitate a special service sheet.

---

28 The South African *Prayer Book* has a special (and clearly penitential) Preface for use where one partner is divorced.
29 A similar situation existed between 1987 and 1994, during the period when women could be deacons but not yet presbyters and could therefore solemnize weddings (as they were experienced ministers) but could not pronounce blessings.